This Coloring Book Belongs To:

____

COOKIE
DOUGH

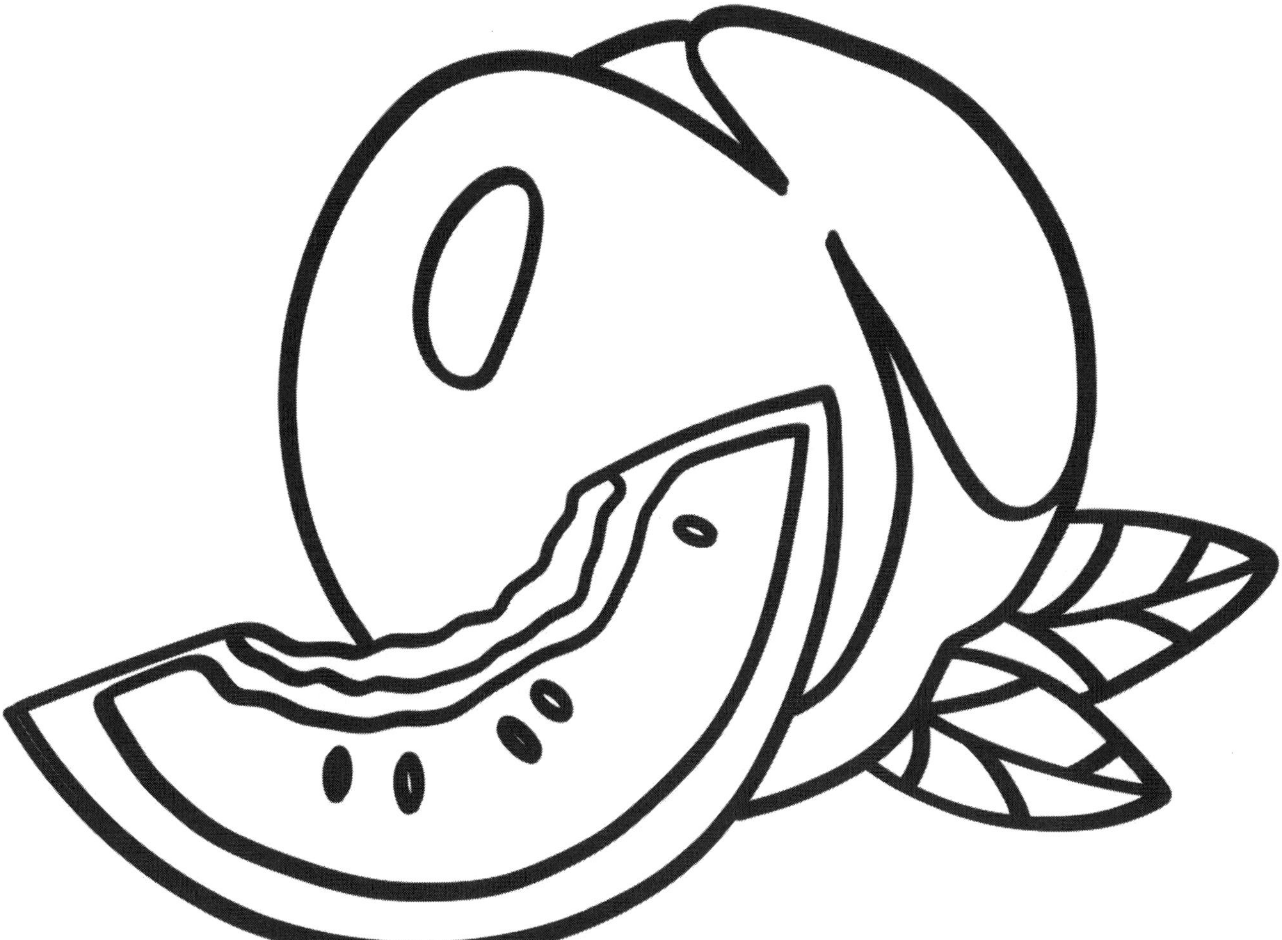

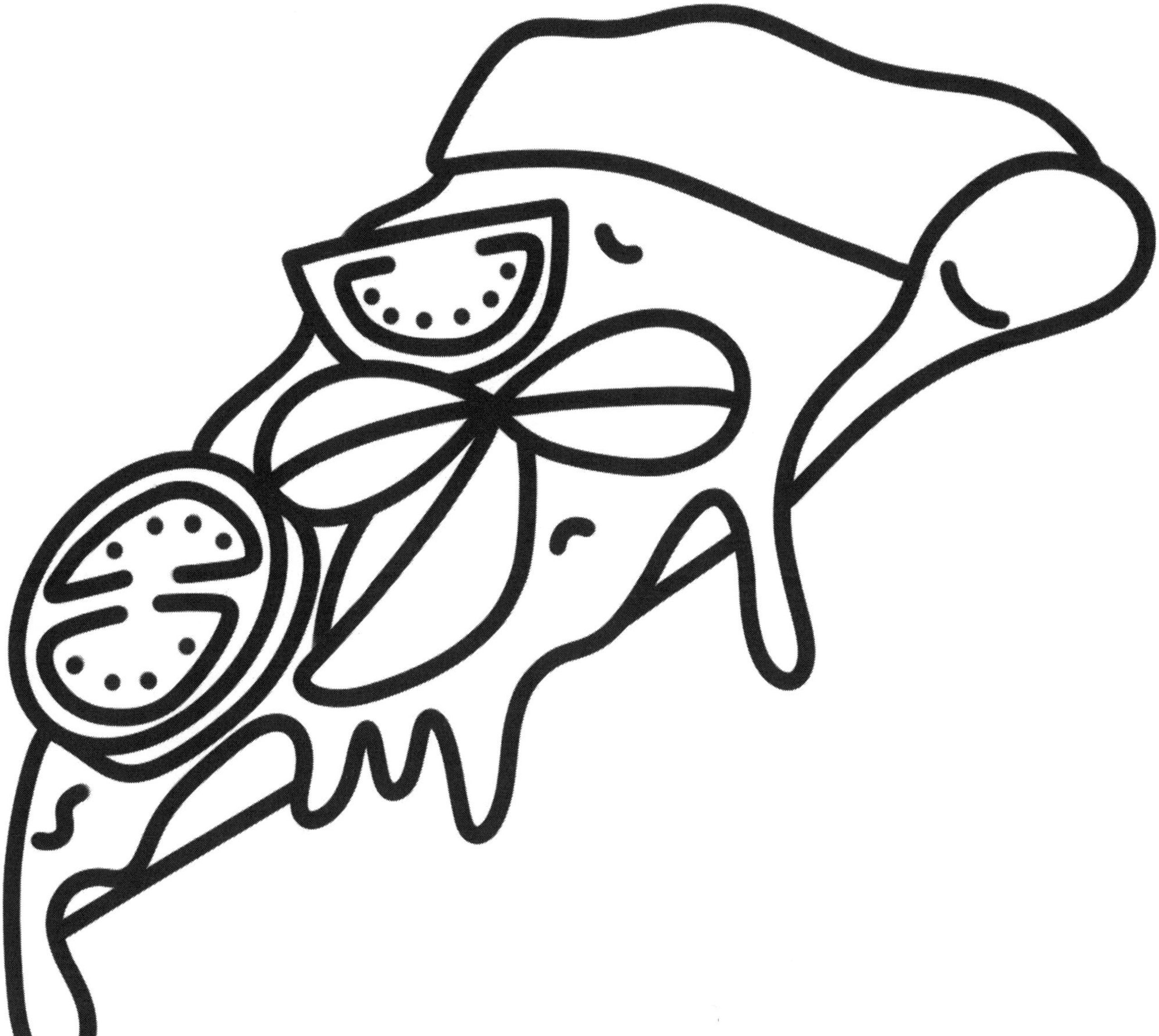

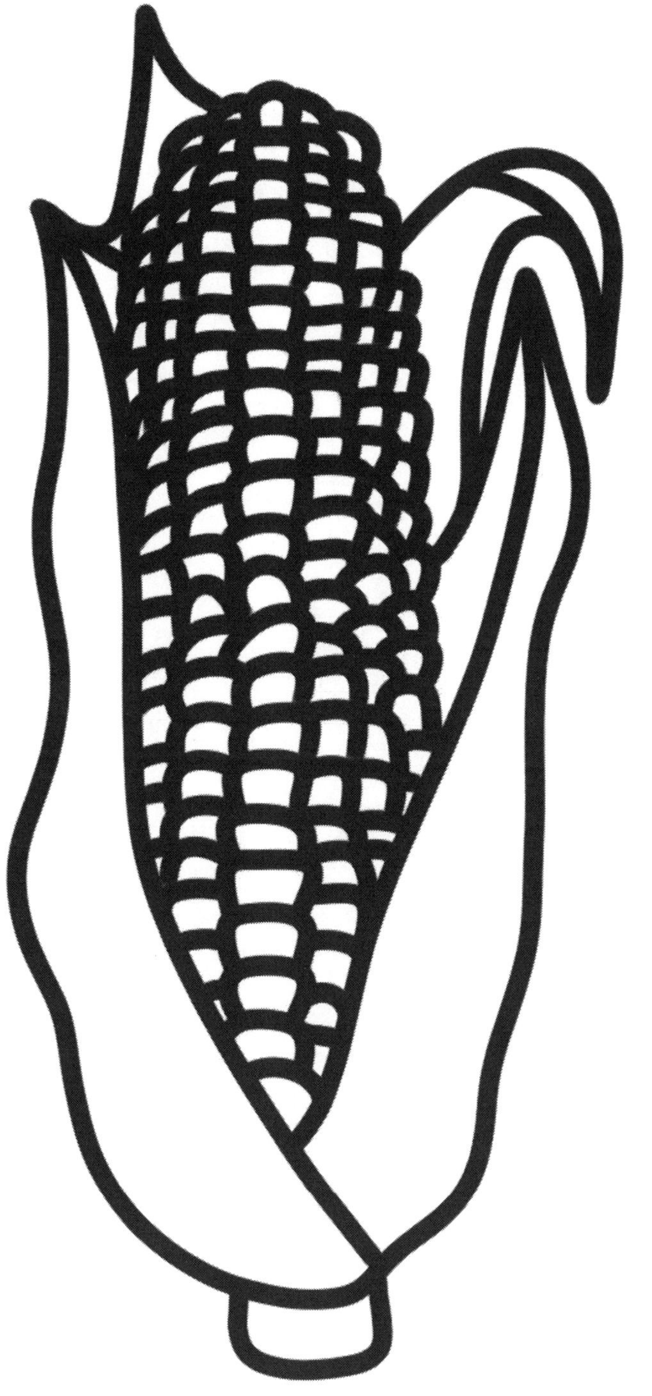

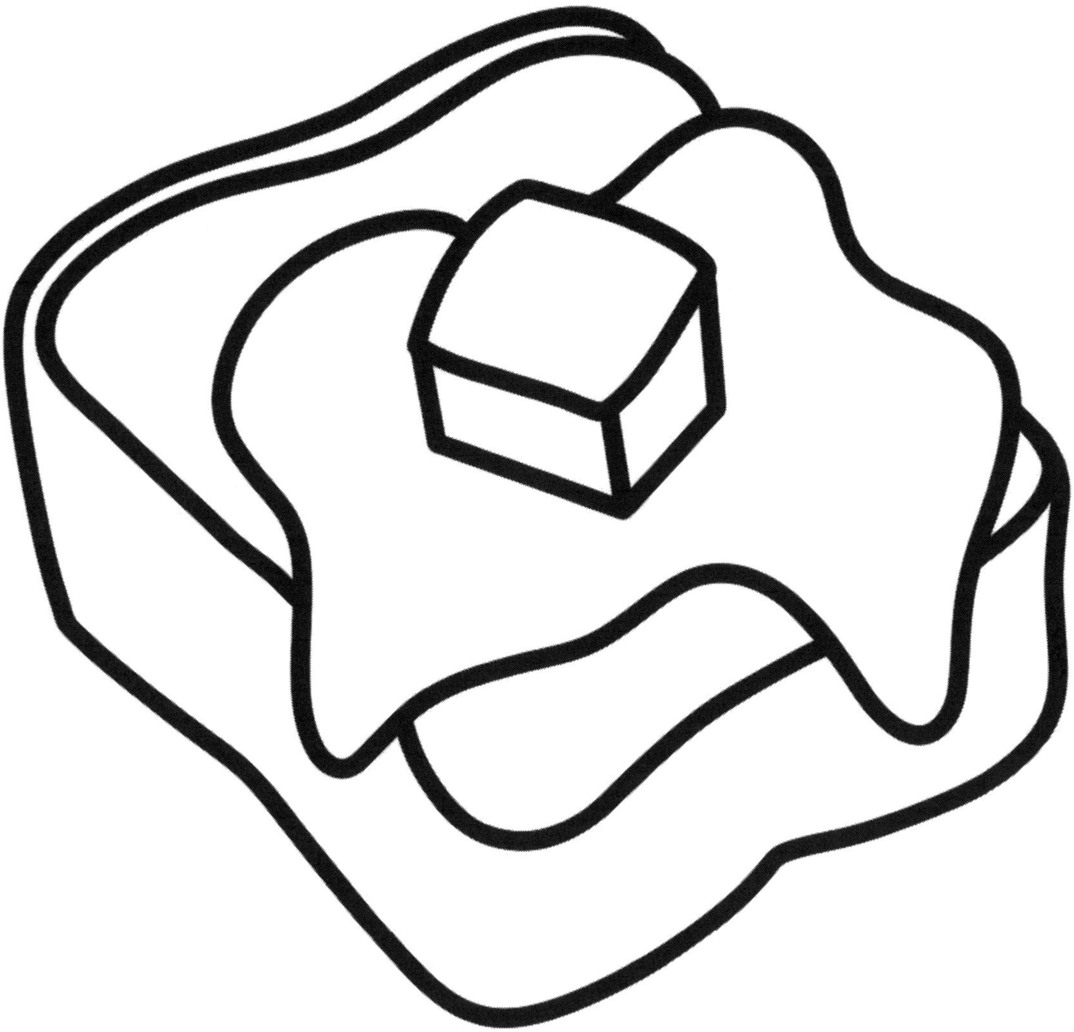

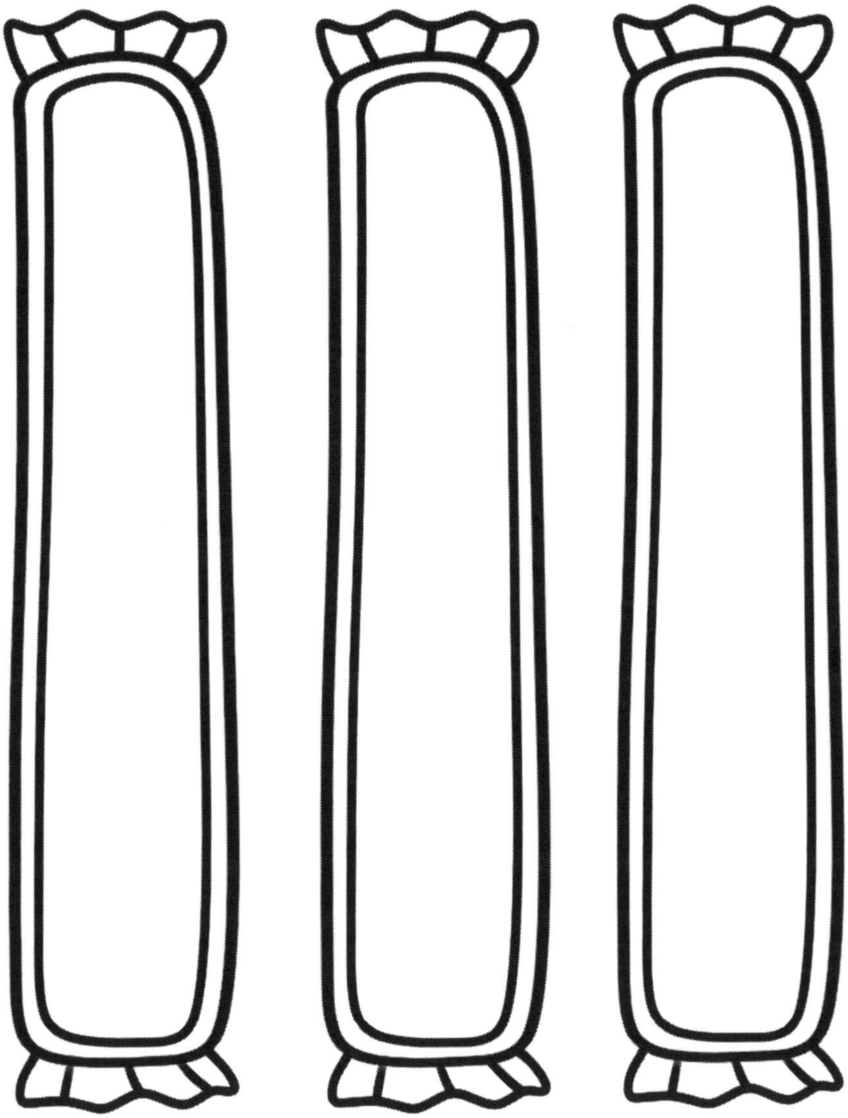

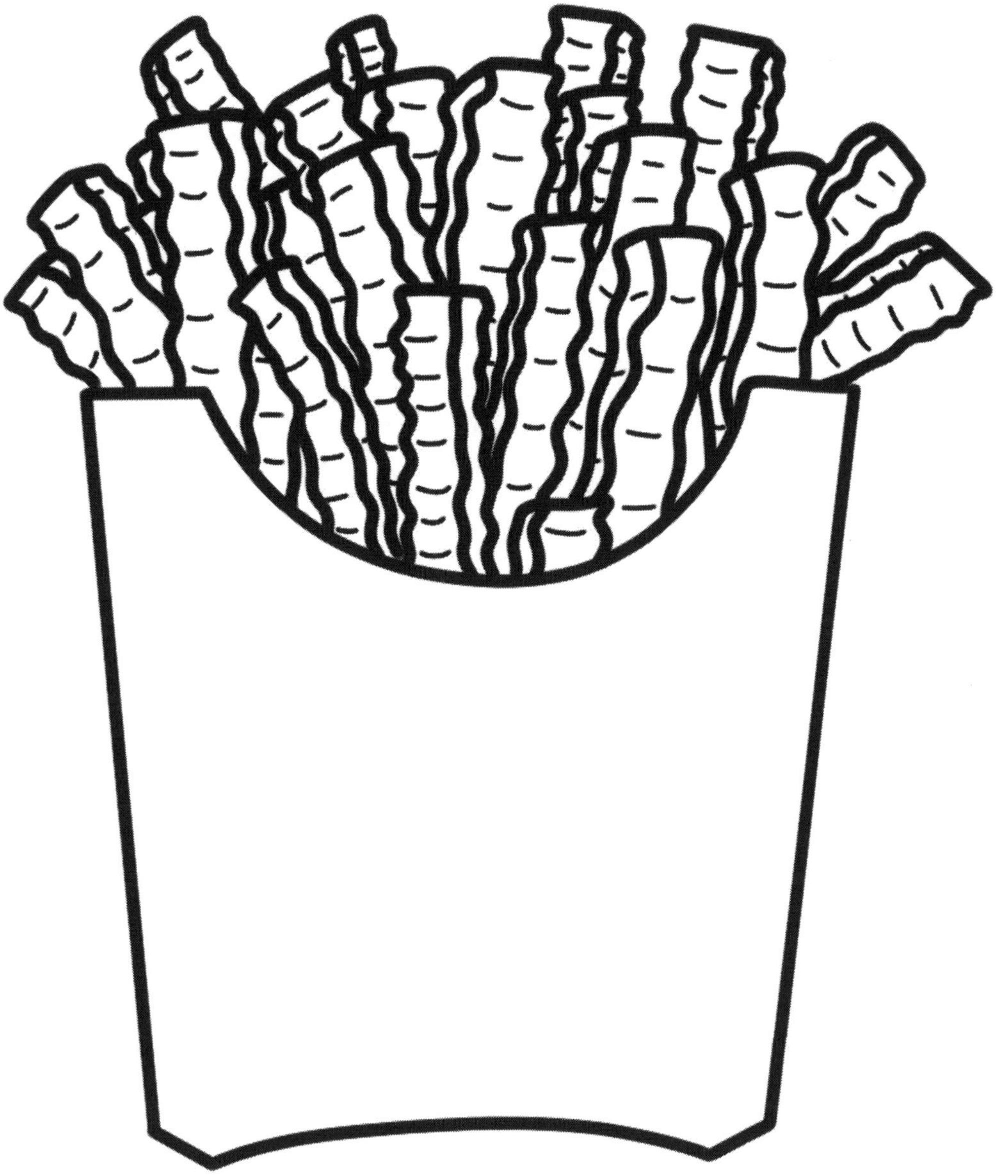

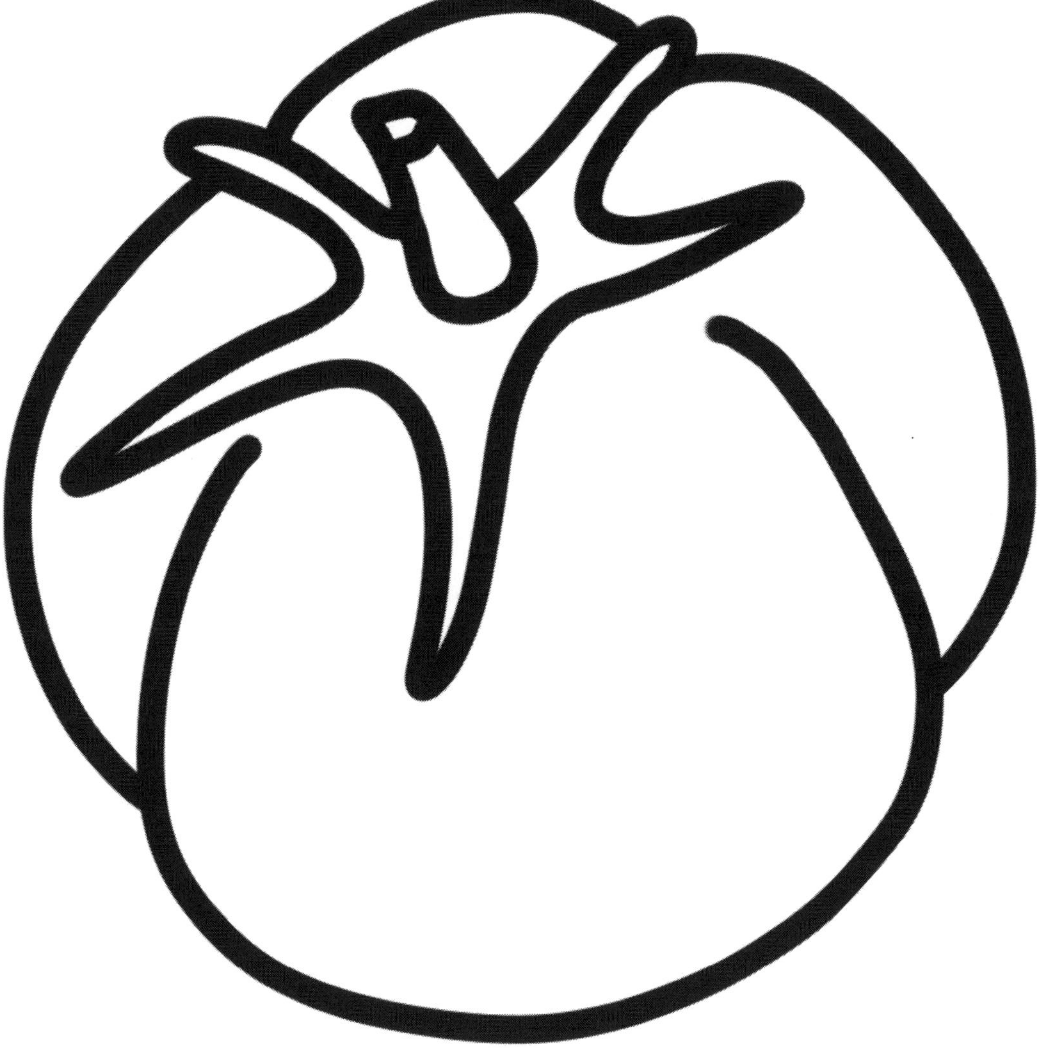

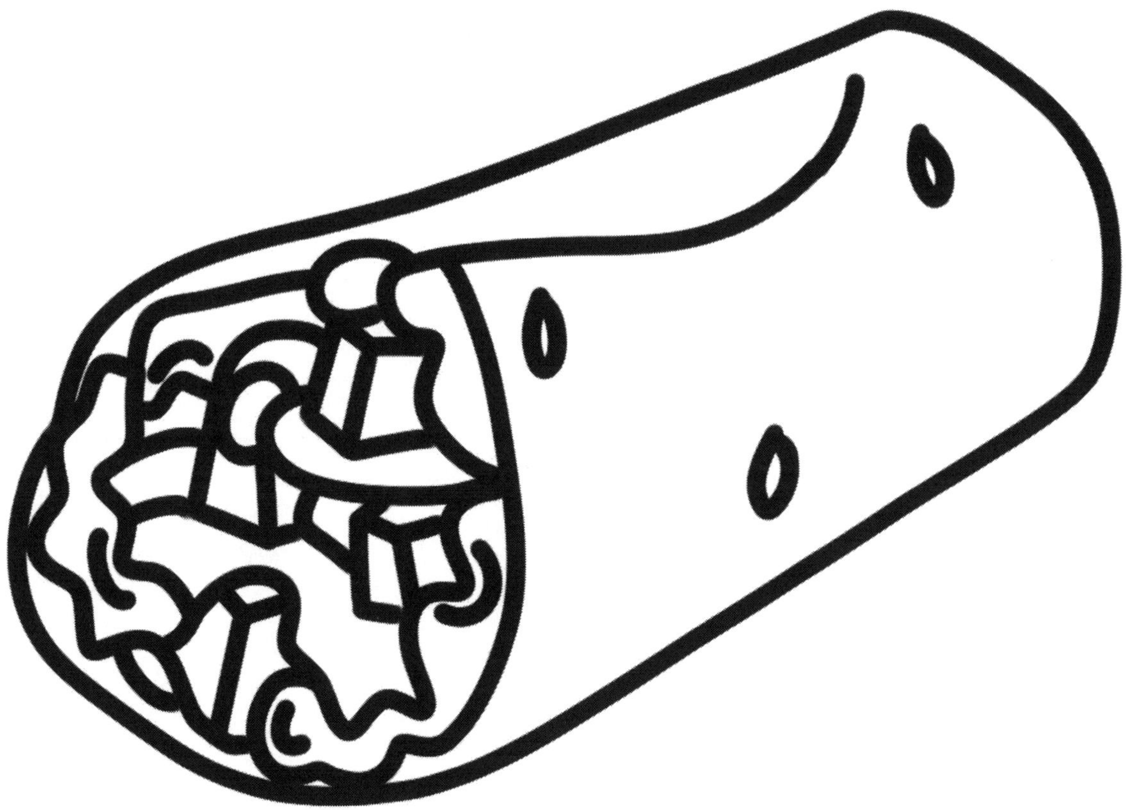

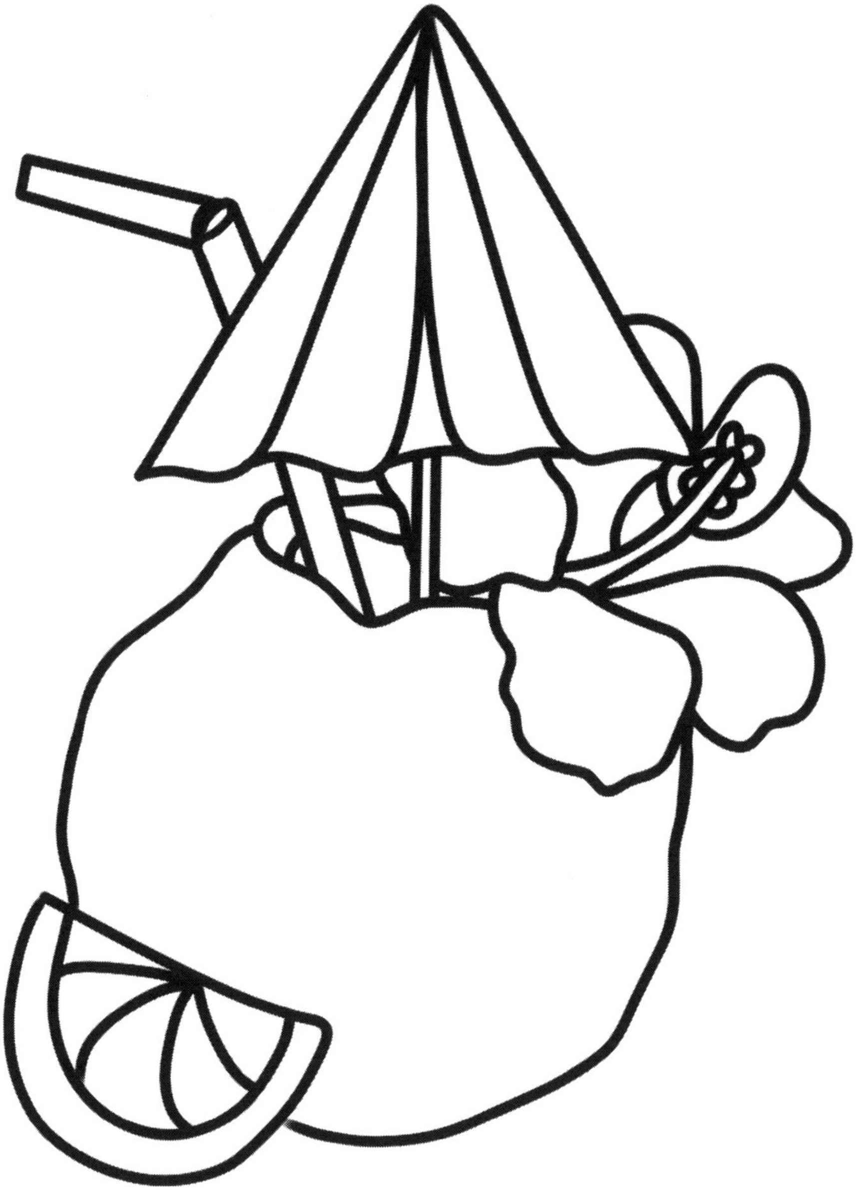

Made in United States
Orlando, FL
03 December 2024

54907483R00048